More cookbooks by Natalie Aul

- Weight Loss Recipes Cookbook Volumes 1-15
- Cooking with Joy 1, 2, & 3
- Weight Loss Recipes Cookbook Whole Food, Plant Based, & Vegan Volume 1, 2, & 3
- Simply Delicious A 14 Day Food Plan
- Weight Loss Recipes Cookbook Holiday Volume
- Batch Cooking Made Easy Cookbook 1 & 2

Special Thanks to:
My sister Kelly, without you this book would not be possible!
My mom Maggie, for your encouragement, and introducing us to this new way of life.
To everyone who has sent me encouraging notes and such lovely reviews of my other cookbook volumes, you have all been so sweet!
And to YOU my recipe family who keeps me inspired and drooling daily.
I give all the glory to God, without Him I can do nothing, He is my guide and inspiration for each of these recipes. He is my encourager to keep reach my goals and beyond!

Printed in the United States of America

RECIPE CONTENTS

Day 1

Day 2

Day 3

Day 4

Day 5

Day 6

Day 7

Day 8

Day 9

Sauces, Seasonings, and Sides

Food addiction is not like other addictions. Most addictions you can stop cold turkey, but you can't exactly do that with food. Most diets fail, are not realistic, or are not sustainable. "Run 20 miles, do 30 burpee's, then hike Mount Everest. You will be skinny in no time!" or "Eat our pre-made food... it tastes like cardboard and you will be starving most of the time." Or "Eat only baked fish and broccoli" or "Take these pills and drink this potion and BAM thin!" These yo-yo diets do not deal with the real problem and you can't live on pills or climb Mount Everest forever... so the weight comes back.

What if I told you there was a better way to lose weight, be healthy, and keep the weight off? You even get to eat a lot of delicious food without starving the whole time! If I can do it, a chunky kid who loved pizza, ice cream, and mac & cheese, you can do it! I will give you all the recipes (that's the hard part). Sugar free, flour free, 3 weighed meals a day (no snacks in between).

Deliciously FREE!

With Joy, Natalie

"Look at me. I stand at the door. I knock. If you hear me call and open the door, I'll come right in and sit down to supper with you. Conquerors will sit alongside me at the head table, just as I, having conquered, took the place of honor at the side of my Father. That's my gift to the conquerors!2
Revelation 3:20-21 MSG

Day 1

BREAKFAST:
1 GRAIN, 1 PROTEIN, 6OZ FRUIT

LUNCH:
1 PROTEIN, 1 FAT, 6OZ FRUIT,
6OZ VEGETABLES

DINNER:
1 PROTEIN, 1 FAT, 14OZ VEGETABLES

From my volume 15 cookbook

PLAN YOUR DAY

Today's Shopping List

- 1 Can pumpkin
- 1 Banana
- Maple extract (my favorite is on amazon)
- Cinnamon
- Sea salt
- 12 Eggs
- 1 32oz Tub plain Greek yogurt
- Old fashion rolled oats
- 1 Can chickpeas
- Garlic powder
- Lemon juice
- Parsley
- Dill
- Broccoli
- Celery
- Carrots
- Cucumber
- 1 Small bag shredded cheddar cheese
- 1 Can black olives
- 2 Spaghetti squash
- 1 Jar spaghetti sauce
- 1 Small tub ricotta cheese
- Basil
- Oregano
- 1 Package turkey bacon
- Fruit for lunch

Urgent

Appointment

Plan ahead or plan to fail

Important Notes

perfect

signs of the island being brought back to life anyway, I had

You are only one thought away from a good day.

Pumpkiney, cinnamoney, cobblerey, deliciousness

Pumpkin Cobbler

INGREDIENTS

- 3oz Canned pumpkin (1/2 fruit)
- 3oz Banana (1/2 fruit)
- 1tsp of each: Maple extract, pumpkin pie spice, cinnamon
- Pinch of Sea salt
- 1 Egg (1/2 protein)
- 4oz Plain Greek yogurt (1/2 protein)
- 1oz Uncooked oats (full grain)

DIRECTIONS

1. Preheat oven to 375.
2. Mash banana.
3. Add maple extract, salt, pumpkin pie spice, pumpkin, egg, 2oz Greek yogurt, and mix.
4. Pour mixture into a lightly oiled baking dish.
5. Top with oats and sprinkle with cinnamon.
6. Bake 45min or until golden.
7. Top with remaining Greek yogurt and a pinch of salt.

Savory pizza, with a ranch sauce, and topped with crunchy vegetables

Vegetable Ranch Pizza

INGREDIENTS

- 3oz Canned chickpeas (1/2 protein)
- 2oz Plain Greek yogurt (1/4 protein)
- Pinch of each: Sea salt, garlic powder, onion power, lemon juice, parsley
- 1/2tsp Dill
- 6oz total: Broccoli, celery, carrots, tomato, onion, cucumber (full vegetable)
- 1oz Shredded cheese (1/2 fat + ¼ protein)
- 1oz Black olives (1/2 fat)

SIDE WITH 6OZ FRUIT FOR A COMPLETE LUNCH.

DIRECTIONS

1. Preheat oven to 375.
2. Drain chickpeas.
3. Using a hand blender, blend chickpeas, 1/2oz cheese, and salt until smooth.
4. Lightly oil a small baking dish.
5. Press chickpea mixture onto pan and bake 25min.
6. In a separate bowl mix yogurt, spices, and lemon juice.
7. Chop/dice vegetables.
8. Top crust with yogurt mixture.
9. Sprinkle with vegetables, olives, and remaining 1/2oz cheese.

Mmm Mmm good! layers of cheesy goodness with crispy bacon.

Spaghetti Squash Lasagna Bowl

INGREDIENTS

- 12oz Cooked spaghetti squash
- 4oz Spaghetti sauce (with the squash = full vegetable + condiment)
- 3oz Ricotta cheese (3/4 protein)
- 1oz Parmesan cheese (full fat)
- Pinch of each: Garlic salt, garlic powder, parsley, basil, oregano, lemon juice
- 1oz Turkey bacon (1/4 protein)

DIRECTIONS

1. Preheat oven to 375.
2. Add bacon to a baking pan and bake 15-20min or until desired crispiness.
3. Slice squash length wise.
4. Scoop out seeds (save seeds for roasting)
5. Drizzle and rub squash with olive oil.
6. Place squash rind side up on a baking sheet and roast 45min.
7. With a fork scrape strands from squash into a large bowl.
8. In a separate bowl mix ricotta, spices, and lemon juice.
9. Spread ricotta mixture into squash.
10. Top with sauce and sprinkle with cheese.

Congratulations! You completed day 1! Day 1 can be the hardest, it can feel overwhelming, and even alien. But don't worry, we all start this way especially when we are starting something new. Just keep at it, you are growing new skills, and habits, and creating a whole new world of food freedom! So, give yourself grace, love, and time to adjust. Today's meals just show that it's not so bad ditching sugar and flour. You can still have exciting and delicious meals. You had cake for breakfast, pizza for lunch, and a delicious lasagna stuffed spaghetti for dinner! You are eating the best!

My Daily Gratitude

Today I'm grateful for

Daily Affirmation

My mind and body are calm and at peace with food

Kindness that I shared today

I learned today

WATER INTAKE

BREAKFAST:
1 GRAIN, 1 PROTEIN, 6OZ FRUIT

LUNCH:
1 PROTEIN, 1 FAT, 6OZ FRUIT,
6OZ VEGETABLES

DINNER:
1 PROTEIN, 1 FAT, 14OZ VEGETABLES

From my volume 11 cookbook

PLAN YOUR DAY

Today's Shopping List

- 1 Bag Puffed Kamut
- 1 16oz Jar Peanut Butter
- 1-2 Bananas
- Instant coffee
- Chai spice (or make your own, find recipe in Sauces, Seasonings, and Sides)
- Colored bell peppers
- 1 Yellow onion
- Broccoli
- Cauliflower
- 1 Package Turley Pepperoni
- 1 Can Black olives
- Shredded cheese
- 1 Can or fresh pineapple
- Everything But the Bagel Seasoning
- Garlic salt
- Parsley
- 1-2 Spaghetti squash
- 1 Jar Spaghetti sauce
- Parmesan cheese
- Lemon juice

Urgent

Appointment

Plan ahead or plan to fail

Important Notes

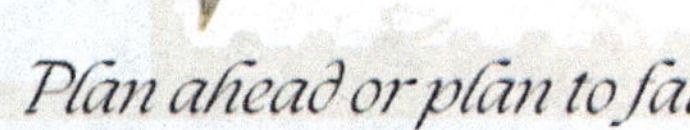

You are only one thought away from a good day.

a perfectly frozen delight for breakfast! You can thaw in the microwave for 30sec if its too hard to eat right away

Frozen Coffee Crispy Bar with Banana Chai Cream

INGREDIENTS

- 1oz Puffed kamut (full grain)
- 1/2tsp Instant coffee
- Pinch of each: Sea salt, maple extract, chai spice, instant coffee
- 1oz Peanut butter (1/2 protein)
- 4oz Plain Greek yogurt (1/2 protein)
- 6oz Banana (full fruit)

DIRECTIONS

1. Mash banana.
2. Mix puffed kamut, 2oz Greek yogurt, maple extract, salt, 3oz banana, and 1/2tsp coffee.
3. Scoop mixture into a mini spring form pan or a Tupperware.
4. In the same bowl mix remaining banana, yogurt, chai spice and a pinch of coffee.
5. Scoop mixture on top of puffed kamut mixture.
6. Drizzle with peanut butter and freeze 3-6hrs or overnight.

This even tastes even better the next day.

Pizza Salad

INGREDIENTS

- 6oz total: Colored peppers, onion, broccoli, cauliflower (full vegetable)
- 1oz Turkey pepperonis (1/4 protein)
- 2oz Black olives (full fat)
- 2oz Plain Greek yogurt (1/4 protein)
- 1oz Cheese (1/2 protein)
- Pinch of each: Oregano, parsley, sea salt, garlic salt, basil, Everything But The Bagel Seasoning
- 6oz Pineapple (full fruit)

DIRECTIONS

1. Dice vegetables.
2. Cube cheese.
3. Cut pepperonis into 4ths.
4. Add all ingredients together and mix.
5. For best flavor refrigerate 30min-overnight.

mmm mmm good! layers of cheesy goodness with crispy bacon.

Left over Spaghetti Squash Lasagna Bowl

INGREDIENTS

- 12oz Cooked spaghetti squash
- 4oz Spaghetti sauce (with the squash = full vegetable + condiment)
- 3oz Ricotta cheese (3/4 protein)
- 1oz Parmesan cheese (full fat)
- Pinch of each: Garlic salt, garlic powder, parsley, basil, oregano, lemon juice
- 1oz Turkey bacon (1/4 protein)

DIRECTIONS

1. With a fork scrape strands from squash into a large bowl.
2. In a separate bowl mix ricotta, spices, and lemon juice.
3. Spread ricotta mixture into squash.
4. Break bacon into small pieces.
5. Top with sauce, bacon, and sprinkle with cheese.

Woohoo for day 2!

Weighing and measuring are starting to make a little more sense now. You're getting the hang of just eating 3 meals with no snacking. You might even notice how many times throughout the day you have had the urge or thought to take a bite or have a snack. Those feelings will disappear as you keep going. I remember a time I was shredding a block of cheese and without even thinking I picked up a pinch of cheese and was about to eat it, I wasn't hungry. It was just an old habit I had created. Thankfully that habit is gone! If I can overcome that habit, so can you!! Congratulations on sticking with it to day 2!!

You've got this!

My Daily Gratitude

Daily Affirmation

I have a strong and healthy metabolism

Today I'm grateful for

Kindness that I shared today

I learned today

WATER INTAKE

BREAKFAST:
1 GRAIN, 1 PROTEIN, 6OZ FRUIT

LUNCH:
1 PROTEIN, 1 FAT, 6OZ FRUIT,
6OZ VEGETABLES

DINNER:
1 PROTEIN, 1 FAT, 14OZ VEGETABLES

From my volume 12 cookbook

PLAN YOUR DAY

Today's Shopping List

- Baking soda
- Baking powder
- 1-2 Banana
- Flax seed
- Riced cauliflower
- 4-8oz Milk
- Chia seeds
- Vanilla extract
- Nutmeg
- 1 8oz Package cream cheese
- 1-2 Apples
- 1 12oz Bag frozen carrots
- 1 12oz Bag frozen broccoli
- 2 12oz Bag frozen green beans
- 1 Yellow onion
- 1 Can chickpeas
- 8oz-16oz Vegetable broth
- Onion powder
- Paprika
- Pepper

Urgent

Appointment

Plan ahead or plan to fail

Important Notes

signs of the island being brought back to life anyway, I had

You are only one thought away from a good day.

Pancakes with a creamy topping

Chai Latte Chickpea Pancakes

INGREDIENTS

- 3oz Canned chickpeas (1/2 protein)
- 1oz Uncooked oats (full grain)
- Pinch of each: Sea salt, maple extract, instant coffee
- 1/4tsp of each: Baking soda, baking powder
- 6oz Banana (full fruit)
- 1/2oz Ground flax seed (1/4 protein)
- 3Tbsp Brewed coffee or water
- 1/2tsp Chai spice*
- 2oz Plain Greek yogurt (1/4 protein)

FIND CHAI SPICE IN "SAUCES, SEASONINGS, AND SIDES."

DIRECTIONS

1. Heat and lightly oil a skillet.
2. Drain and blend chickpeas with a hand blender or food processor until smooth.
3. Add 3oz banana, chai spice, salt, maple extract, oats, instant coffee, brewed coffee, ground flax seed, baking soda, and baking powder to chickpeas and mash/mix.
4. Scoop 1/4th of mixture into skillet and cook 3-5min.
5. Flip and cook another 2-4min.
6. Repeat with remaining batter.
7. In a separate bowl mash 3oz banana, instant coffee, yogurt, salt, another pinch of chai spice, and mix.
8. Top pancakes with yogurt mixture.

Connamon-y delicious!

Cinnamon Roll Porridge

INGREDIENTS

- 6oz Riced cauliflower (full vegetable)
- 4oz Milk (1/2 protein)
- 1/2oz total: Ground flax seed, chia seeds (1/4 protein)
- Pinch of each: Sea salt, allspice, maple extract, vanilla extract
- 2tsp Cinnamon
- 1/4tsp Nutmeg
- 3oz Banana (1/2 fruit)
- 1oz Cream cheese (full fat)
- 2oz Plain Greek yogurt (1/4 protein)
- 3oz Apples (1/2 fruit)

DIRECTIONS

1. Add milk to a pot.
2. Heat over medium heat.
3. Add cauliflower and bring to a boil.
4. Reduce heat and simmer 5min.
5. Add spices.
6. Mash banana and add to pot.
7. Add flax and chia seeds, yogurt, and cream cheese.
8. Mix and remove from heat.
9. Slice apples.
10. Top with apples and a sprinkle more of cinnamon

Crispy topping? Oh yes!

Green Bean Casserole
X2

INGREDIENTS

- 2lbs total: Green beans, peas, carrots, broccoli (plus onion = full vegetable)
- 2oz Onion
- 2oz Turkey bacon (1/4 protein)
- 4oz Plain Greek yogurt (1/4 protein)
- 3oz Canned chickpeas (1/4 protein)
- 3oz Cheese (1/4 protein + full fat)
- 8oz Vegetable broth (condiment up to 8oz free)
- 1tsp of each: Onion powder, parsley
- Pinch of each: Sea salt, pepper, paprika, garlic salt

DIRECTIONS

1. Preheat oven to 350.
2. Blend chickpeas, salt, onion, and paprika until smooth.
3. Stir in 1/2oz of cheese.
4. Lightly oil a large baking dish. In a separate bowl, mix yogurt, onion powder, garlic salt, salt, pepper, parsley, remaining cheese, and broth.
5. Layer vegetables in the baking dish.
6. Pour yogurt mixture on top.
7. Crumble chickpea mixture and bacon on top.
8. Cover and bake 45min-1hr.
9. Uncover and bake 10-15min or until top is golden brown.
10. Divide casserole into 2 servings. 1/2 = full dinner

Wow you have already completed day 3! Give yourself a round of applause. You are doing it! At this point, you might be struggling with some hunger feelings or stronger desires to snack at night time. (I used to be a huge nighttime snacker.) When those desires come it could actually be a sense of thirst or I call it fake brain hunger. It's not real. Your brain is just used to entertaining itself with eating. Instead, have a nice tea or a sugar-free bubbly/soda. There are many many many flavor options for hot and cold teas. This will quench your thirst and give your brain a little relief. If you're tempted at night, just remember the delicious breakfast you will have waiting for you in the morning! These desires will dissipate as you keep going.

My Daily Gratitude

Daily Affirmation

I am thankful, grateful, and kind

Today I'm grateful for

Kindness that I shared today

I learned today

WATER INTAKE

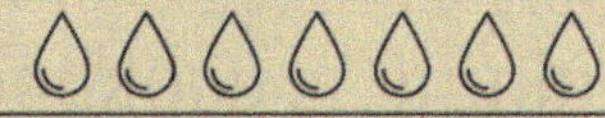

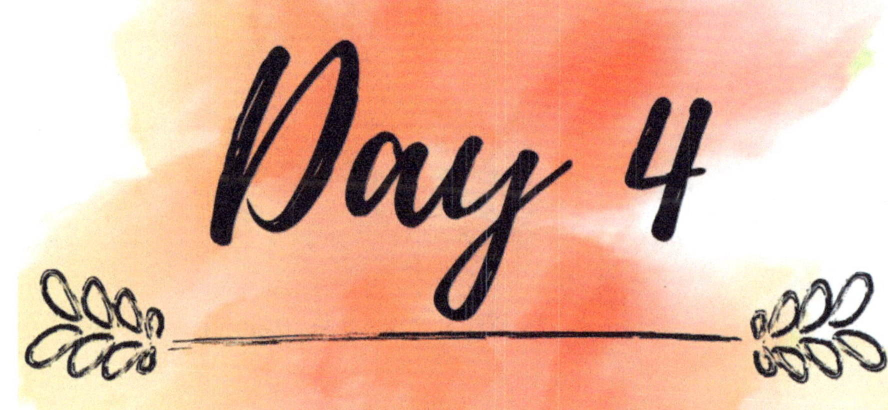

BREAKFAST:
1 GRAIN, 1 PROTEIN, 6OZ FRUIT

LUNCH:
1 PROTEIN, 1 FAT, 6OZ FRUIT,
6OZ VEGETABLES

DINNER:
1 PROTEIN, 1 FAT, 14OZ VEGETABLES

From my volume 13 cookbook

PLAN YOUR DAY

Today's Shopping List

- 1 Banana
- 1 Can Pineapple
- 1 Bag Baby Carrots
- Ground cloves
- Raw or oven roasted Walnuts
- Chicken breast
- 1 Bag coleslaw
- Spring mix lettuce
- 1 Onion
- Cherry tomatoes
- Colored bell pepper
- 2 Apples
- Toasted sesame oil or sesame oil
- Ground ginger
- Garlic powder
- Sesame seeds
- Apple cider vinegar

Urgent

Appointment

Plan ahead or plan to fail

Important Notes

signs of the island being brought back to life anyway, I had

You are only one thought away from a good day.

Mini carrot cakes! Tastes delicious
and they are so cute!

Carrot Cake Muffins

INGREDIENTS

- 1 Egg (1/2 protein)
- 2oz Banana (1/3 fruit)
- 2oz Pineapple (1/3 fruit)
- 2oz Carrots (1/3 fruit)
- 1oz Uncooked oats (full grain)
- 1/4tsp Baking soda
- 1/2tsp of each: Cinnamon, nutmeg
- Pinch of each: Cloves, sea salt, vanilla extract
- 1/2oz Peanut butter (1/4 protein)
- 1/2oz Walnuts (1/4 protein)

DIRECTIONS

1. Preheat oven to 350.
2. Line or lightly oil a mini muffin pan or a regular muffin pan.
3. Mash banana.
4. Shred carrots.
5. Add pineapple, shredded carrots, oats, baking soda, seasoning, to mashed banana and mix.
6. Pour mixture into muffin pan and bake 25-30min or until a toothpick comes out clean.
7. Top with peanut butter and walnuts.

Layers of textures and delicious asian flavor

Grilled Chicken Asian Salad with Sesame Ginger Dressing

INGREDIENTS

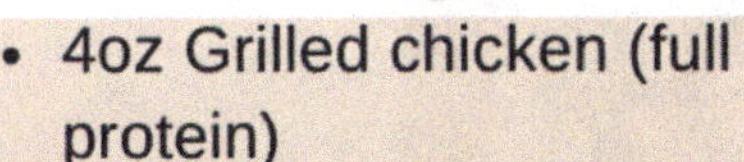

- 4oz Grilled chicken (full protein)
- 6oz total: Cole slaw mix, spring mix lettuce, onion, cherry tomato, colored peppers (full vegetable)
- 6oz total: Apple, pineapple (full fruit)

-Sesame Ginger Dressing

- 1Tbsp Toasted sesame oil (full fat)
- 1tsp Ginger
- 1/2tsp of each: Onion powder, garlic powder
- Pinch of each: Sea salt, sesame seeds
- 1oz Apple cider vinegar

DIRECTIONS

1. Chop/slice vegetables, fruit, and chicken.
2. Layer lettuce, coleslaw mix, vegetables, fruit, and chicken in a large bowl.
3. Add all of the dressing ingredients to a bowl and whisk.
4. Drizzle with Sesame Ginger Dressing

Remaining 1/2 of Green Bean Casserole for dinner

You crushed day 4!!!

Isn't it nice to have leftovers for dinner? I almost quit because I was feeling overwhelmed with all the cooking we had to do every single day! But then we figured out the trick of making dinner enough for 2 days at a time. There was such a lovely relief with just having leftovers. It still might feel like a shock having to cook all of your meals, but in reality, how much time did we waste thinking, shopping, and plotting our next hit of a sugary treat? Just trying to figure out what will "hit the spot" and it never did. It will always leave you wanting more. It might satisfy for what, 3 minutes? 5 minutes? Then you will just want more and more and more! Remember this when food is trying to lie to you with "I will solve your problems, make you feel better, make the hurt and cravings go away." LIES!!! Food can't solve one thing.

My Daily Gratitude

Today I'm grateful for

Daily Affirmation

I am strong and energetic

Kindness that I shared today

I learned today

WATER INTAKE

Something I am looking forward to tomorrow
habits I would like to change
New habits I would like to add
Kindness I can show tomorrow
Something I want to learn

BREAKFAST:
1 GRAIN, 1 PROTEIN, 6OZ FRUIT

LUNCH:
1 PROTEIN, 1 FAT, 6OZ FRUIT,
6OZ VEGETABLES

DINNER:
1 PROTEIN, 1 FAT, 14OZ VEGETABLES

From my volume 13 cookbook

PLAN YOUR DAY

Today's Shopping List

- Crunchy peanut butter
- 2 Banana
- Allspice
- Almond extract
- Frozen blueberries
- Frozen raspberries
- Cucumber
- Celery
- 1 32oz Tub Plain Greek yogurt
- Grapes
- Canned chicken or use left over grilled chicken
- Unsweetened coconut flakes
- Raw or oven roasted pecans
- Quinoa
- Turkey bacon
- Shredded cheese
- 2 12oz Frozen broccoli
- 2 12oz Frozen asparagus
- 2 12oz Frozen carrots
- 4-8oz Milk

Urgent

Appointment

Plan ahead or plan to fail

Important Notes

signs of the island being brought back to life anyway. I had

You are only one thought away from a good day.

One giant, thick, cookie for breakfast!

Frittata Cookie

INGREDIENTS

- 2oz Crunchy Peanut butter (full protein)
- 1oz Uncooked oats (full grain)
- 4oz Banana (2/3 fruit)
- Pinch of each: Sea salt, baking soda, allspice, clove, instant coffee, almond extract
- 3/4tsp Cinnamon
- 1/4tsp of each: nutmeg, ginger
- 2oz total: Frozen blueberries, raspberries (1/3 fruit)

DIRECTIONS

1. Heat and lightly oil a skillet to med/low heat.
2. Mash banana.
3. Add remaining ingredients except blueberries and raspberries to banana and mix.
4. Spread mixture into one big cookie in skillet.
5. Let cook 5-7min or until top is set and not glossy.
6. In a separate bowl microwave berries 1min.
7. Top cookie with berries.

Coconutty and oh so yummy!

Tropical Coconut Chicken Slaw

INGREDIENTS

- 6oz total: Coleslaw mix, celery, cucumber, onion (full vegetable)
- 4oz Plain Greek yogurt (1/2 protein)
- 3oz Grapes (1/2 fruit)
- 3oz Pineapple (1/2 fruit)
- 1oz Canned chicken (1/4 protein)
- 1/2oz Unsweetened coconut flakes (full fat)
- 1/2oz Pecans (1/4 protein)
- Pinch of Sea salt

DIRECTIONS

1. Dice/chop vegetables and fruit.
2. Add all ingredients to a bowl and toss/mix.

Cheesy heaven

Quinoa Cheese Sauce and Veggies

INGREDIENTS

- 2oz Cooked quinoa (1/2 protein)
- 2oz Milk (1/4 protein)
- 1oz Turkey bacon (1/4 protein)
- 1oz Shredded cheese (full fat)
- 2-3Tbsp Hot water
- Sea salt
- 14oz total: Roasted broccoli, steamed asparagus, roasted carrots (weigh after cooking) (full vegetable)

DIRECTIONS

1. Add quinoa and milk to a mug, microwave 1min.
2. Add cheese and stir until melted.
3. Add hot water and stir until desired consistency.
4. Add vegetables to a large bowl or plate.
5. Top with cheese sauce, bacon, and sea salt.

And day 5 was a hit!!

This might be where the detox symptoms set in. Don't be alarmed, they can be different for everyone but they will go away. You might feel overwhelmed, the luster and excitement of starting something new might be fading, life may seem harder at the moment, there might be some brain fog, achy joints, headache, tiredness, a little extra crabby, touchy, or emotional, etc. This is normal! One thing that is good about a tougher detox is that you can remember all of these feelings the next time sugar and flour come around wanting to tempt you. Do you want to go through this detox again? I know I don't! That lying treat is not worth the detox that comes after!

You are doing so good, 5 days done!!

YOU CAN DO THIS!!!

My Daily Gratitude

Daily Affirmation

I have the best and most healthy relationships

Today I'm grateful for

Kindness that I shared today

I learned today

WATER INTAKE

BREAKFAST:
1 GRAIN, 1 PROTEIN, 6OZ FRUIT

LUNCH:
1 PROTEIN, 1 FAT, 6OZ FRUIT,
6OZ VEGETABLES

DINNER:
1 PROTEIN, 1 FAT, 14OZ VEGETABLES

From my volume 14 cookbook

PLAN YOUR DAY

Today's Shopping List

- 1-2 Banana
- Coconut extract. My favorite is on amazon
- 1 Can chickpeas
- 1 Banana
- Frozen or fresh strawberries
- Frozen or fresh cherries
- Vegetables for lunch

Urgent

Appointment

Plan ahead or plan to fail

Important Notes

You are only one thought away from a good day.

Fruity, coconutty, and frosted?!
you cant go wrong!

Blueberry Coconut Donuts

INGREDIENTS

- 1 Egg (1/2 protein)
- 3oz Banana (1/2 fruit)
- 3oz Frozen blueberries (1/2 fruit)
- 1oz Uncooked oats (full grain)
- 1/4tsp Baking powder
- Pinch of each: Sea salt, nutmeg
- 1/2tsp Coconut extract
- 4oz Plain Greek yogurt (1/2 protein)

DON'T HAVE A DONUT PAN OR MAKER? DON'T WORRY, YOU CAN MAKE THESE AS MUFFINS!

DIRECTIONS

1. Pre-heat oven 350 or donut maker.
2. Lightly oil donut maker or donut pan.
3. Mash banana.
4. Add egg, 2oz blueberries, 2oz Greek yogurt, oats, baking powder, salt, coconut extract and mix.
5. Scoop mixture into donut maker or donut pan.
6. Cook 10min in maker or bake 25-30min.
7. In a separate bowl microwave 1oz blueberries 1min.
8. Add Greek yogurt to blueberries and mix.
9. Top donuts with yogurt blueberry mixture and a pinch of nutmeg.

Perfect crust with a creamy and fruity filling

Fruit Pizza

INGREDIENTS

- 3oz Chickpeas (1/2 protein)
- 1/2oz Peanut butter (1/4 protein)
- 1oz Banana (1/6 fruit)
- Pinch of each: Sea salt, almond extract, vanilla extract
- 2oz Plain Greek yogurt (1/4 protein)
- 1oz Cream cheese (full fat)
- 5oz total: Blueberries, strawberries, cherries (5/6 fruit)

SIDE WITH 6OZ VEGETABLES FOR A COMPLETE LUNCH.

DIRECTIONS

1. Preheat oven to 350.
2. Drain and blend chickpeas, peanut butter, salt, almond extract with a hand blender or food processor until smooth.
3. Mash banana.
4. Mix banana into chickpea mixture.
5. Press mixture into a lightly oiled or parchment paper lined pie tin or a medium baking dish.
6. Bake 10-15min.
7. In a separate bowl mix yogurt, cream cheese, salt, vanilla.
8. Spread yogurt mixture onto crust and top with fruit.

Cheesy heaven

Quinoa Cheese Sauce and Veggies

INGREDIENTS

- 2oz Cooked quinoa (1/2 protein)
- 2oz Milk (1/4 protein)
- 1oz Turkey bacon (1/4 protein)
- 1oz Shredded cheese (full fat)
- 2-3Tbsp Hot water
- Sea salt
- 14oz total: Roasted broccoli, steamed asparagus, roasted carrots (weigh after cooking) (full vegetable)

DIRECTIONS

1. Add quinoa and milk to a mug, microwave 1min.
2. Add cheese and stir until melted.
3. Add hot water and stir until desired consistency.
4. Add vegetables to a large bowl or plate.
5. Top with cheese sauce, bacon, and sea salt.

6 days completed! Only one more day and you will have completed a whole week! Look at how far you have come. Real sustainable weight loss is not a sprint, it's an endurance run. It's a daily practice. You have to find something you can do every day, day in and day out. If you can do this for 6 days, you can do this for the long haul! That's the difference with this way of eating compared to all the fad diets we have tried and failed. This way of eating will become your new "normal" and "default." If you do mess up, you won't do the crash-and-burn effect of, "Well...I blew this meal, might as well keep going..." No! You're going to say, "Oops I messed up here...oh well, back to normal with the next meal." No matter how many times you fall, fail, or mess up, if you just keep getting back up, brush yourself off, and keep going, you will win every time!

My Daily Gratitude

Daily Affirmation

I am fit, firm, and healthy

Today I'm grateful for

Kindness that I shared today

I learned today

WATER INTAKE

BREAKFAST:
1 GRAIN, 1 PROTEIN, 6OZ FRUIT

LUNCH:
1 PROTEIN, 1 FAT, 6OZ FRUIT,
6OZ VEGETABLES

DINNER:
1 PROTEIN, 1 FAT, 14OZ VEGETABLES

From my volume 7 cookbook

PLAN YOUR DAY

Today's Shopping List

- 1-2 Banana
- 1 Small tub ricotta cheese
- 2 Apples
- Raw or oven roasted peanuts
- Chia seeds
- Hemp seeds
- 4 Cloves garlic
- 2 Onions
- 2 15oz Can tomatoes
- 2 12oz Frozen cauliflower rice
- 2 Green peppers
- 2lbs Carton vegetable broth
- Ground cumin
- Chili powder (Ancho chili is the mildest)
- Chicken breast
- 1 Can great northern beans
- Parsley
- 2-3 Avocados
- Lime juice
- Vegetables for lunch

Urgent

Appointment

Plan ahead or plan to fail

Important Notes

signs of the island being brought back to life anyway, I had

You are only one thought away from a good day.

BERRILICIOUS!

Berrylicious Ricotta Crepes

INGREDIENTS

- 1 Egg (1/2 protein)
- 3oz Banana (1/2 fruit)
- Pinch of each: Baking powder, cinnamon, nutmeg, vanilla extract
- 2oz Ricotta cheese (1/2 protein)
- 1oz Uncooked oats (full grain)
- 3oz Frozen Berries (1/2 fruit)
- Water

DIRECTIONS

1. Heat and lightly oil a skillet.
2. Mash banana.
3. Whisk egg, mashed banana, vanilla, baking powder, cinnamon, and nutmeg.
4. Pour 1/3 of egg mixture into a skillet and tilt the skillet to make 1 thin crepe, you can also use your spatula to lightly spread your egg mixture.
5. Cook 1-2min, flip and cook 1min more.
6. Repeat with remaining egg mixture.
7. In a separate bowl, mix uncooked oats, frozen berries, vanilla, and enough water to cover mixture.
8. Microwave 2min.
9. Top crepes with oat berry mixture, ricotta, and cinnamon.

Apples loaded with heavenly
peanut butter goodness!

Loaded Apples

INGREDIENTS

- 6oz Apples (full fruit)
- 1oz Peanut butter (1/2 protein)
- 1/2oz Toasted unsweetened coconut (full fat)
- 1oz total: Peanuts, pecans, chia seeds, hemp seeds, walnuts (1/2 protein)
- Sea salt

DIRECTIONS

1. Slice apples into discs, remove and discards apple seeds and stems.
2. Top apple discs with peanut butter, nuts, coconut, and sprinkle with salt.

SIDE WITH 6OZ VEGETABLES FOR A COMPLETE LUNCH

Seasoned to perfection!

Southwest Soup x2

INGREDIENTS

- 4 Cloves garlic
- 2lbs total: Onion, canned tomato, green pepper, cauliflower rice (full vegetable)
- 16oz Vegetable broth (condiment up to 8oz free)
- 1/2tsp Chili power
- 1/2tsp Cumin
- 1/4tsp of each: Onion powder, garlic powder
- 4oz Cooked chicken (1/2 protein)
- 6oz Canned great northern beans (1/2 protein)
- Sea salt, pepper
- 1Tbsp Parsley
- 4oz Avocado (full fat)
- 1Tbsp Lime juice

DIRECTIONS

1. Dice/chop vegetables and garlic.
2. Sauté onion, garlic, and peppers in a medium pot.
3. Add broth, spices, chicken, beans, and remaining vegetables.
4. Bring to a boil.
5. Reduce heat and simmer 10-12min until vegetables are tender.
6. Divide soup into 2 servings.
7. Top each serving with avocado, lime juice and salt. (wait to top second serving until after you reheat it so your avocado doesn't turn brown)

Woohoo 7 days completed!!!

One whole week! Now that you have completed one week, what's one more? This next week will be easier and easier as the days go on. Things will start to make sense and click in your brain. The detox symptoms and cravings will start to disappear more and more. This is all downhill (easier) now. With anything in life, it's a journey, but journeys are more fun with friends. This is a perfect time to reach out to a whole community of others who are living the sugar and flour free life and are very supportive. We have over 47,000 members now and still growing on Facebook. Check out "Recipe Ideas. No sugar, no flour, made easy" on Facebook. Also, Follow me on Facebook, Instagram, TikTok, YouTube, and Pinterest. I am more than willing to help with questions in any way that I can

@Weight Loss Recipes Cookbook

My Daily Gratitude

Today I'm grateful for

Daily Affirmation

Everything I do is a success

Kindness that I shared today

I learned today

WATER INTAKE

BREAKFAST:
1 GRAIN, 1 PROTEIN, 6OZ FRUIT

LUNCH:
1 PROTEIN, 1 FAT, 6OZ FRUIT,
6OZ VEGETABLES

DINNER:
1 PROTEIN, 1 FAT, 14OZ VEGETABLES

From my volume 7 cookbook

PLAN YOUR DAY

Today's Shopping List

- 1-2 Banana
- 1 Can hominy
- Turkey pepperoni
- Dijon mustard
- 1 Grapefruit

Urgent

Appointment

Plan ahead or plan to fail

Important Notes

signs of the island being brought back to life anyway, I had

You are only one thought away from a good day.

Yummy Rice crispy bites! And they are super cute!!

Rice Crispberry Bites

INGREDIENTS

- 3oz Banana (1/2 fruit)
- 1 1/2oz Peanut butter (3/4 protein)
- 1oz Puffed kamut (full grain)
- 2oz Plain Greek yogurt (1/4 protein)
- 3oz Frozen blueberries (1/2 fruit)
- Splash of Vanilla extract

CAN'T FIND PUFFED KAMUT? YOU CAN USE 1OZ UNCOOKED OATS INSTEAD

DIRECTIONS

1. Mash banana.
2. Add peanut butter, puffed kamut and mix.
3. Scoop mixture into a mini muffin tin or make into cookie shape or make into one big rice crispy bar.
4. In a separate bowl, microwave blueberries and vanilla 2min.
5. Mix thawed blueberries and yogurt.
6. Top Peanut butter mixture with blueberry yogurt mixture.
7. Freeze 3hrs-overnight.

Oh yes cheese!

Mac and Hominy

INGREDIENTS

- 6oz Hominy (full vegetable)
- 2oz Ricotta cheese (full fat)
- 2oz Plain Greek yogurt (1/4 protein)
- 1oz Cheese (1/2 protein)
- 1oz Turkey pepperoni (1/4 protein)
- Pinch of each: Onion powder, garlic powder, basil, sea salt, pepper, Dijon mustard
- 1 Grapefruit (full fruit)

DIRECTIONS

1. Add all ingredients except pepperonis to a small saucepan.
2. Heat over medium/low heat.
3. Simmer (but do not boil) 7-10min until everything is nice and hot.
4. Pour mac and hominy into a bowl and top with pepperoni.

Leftovers for dinner!

You are rocking this new lifestyle! You might be having some mixed emotions at this point, and guess what it is? Grief. Yes, grief. Grieving the foods you no longer eat, grieving your old lifestyle and habits, and grieving the changes you have to make. It's normal. We all go through this process. In this time of grieving, it's time to discover new ways of rewarding yourself instead of food. It might be a shopping trip (I know I did some online shopping, maybe not even buying things, but just…shopping), a spa day, gifting yourself with an item you have always wanted to get, maybe getting together with friends, going on a day trip to somewhere fun, watching your favorite movie, taking a nap, starting a new hobby, or maybe help someone else, etc. I remember after I passed my bus drivers test, the usual celebration used to be getting pizza, ice cream, and a good movie. After I passed, we drove home and my sister surprised me with a balloon and a new beautiful bracelet. That meant more to me than any junk food! I still have that bracelet and every time I wear it I am reminded of that special moment. You don't need someone to surprise you. You can treat yourself if you need to. Now, take the time to think of the things you really enjoy in life. Another thing I have found that brings me joy is serving and loving others. Whether it's serving Thanksgiving dinner at church, or surprising my family with little gifts for Valentine's Day without expecting anything in return, those are lasting memories that are WAY better than food!

My Daily Gratitude

Daily Affirmation

I am at the right place at the right time

Today I'm grateful for

Kindness that I shared today

I learned today

WATER INTAKE

BREAKFAST:
1 GRAIN, 1 PROTEIN, 6OZ FRUIT

LUNCH:
1 PROTEIN, 1 FAT, 6OZ FRUIT,
6OZ VEGETABLES

DINNER:
1 PROTEIN, 1 FAT, 14OZ VEGETABLES

From my volume 8 cookbook

PLAN YOUR DAY

Today's Shopping List

- Shredded wheat
- 1 32oz Tub plain Greek yogurt
- Oven roasted sunflower kernels
- Raw or oven roasted cashews
- Raw or oven roasted macadamia nuts
- 1 Banana
- Frozen strawberries
- 2-3 Tomatoes
- 1 Can tuna
- Mayo
- Block cheddar cheese
- Pickles
- 2-3 Onions
- Celery
- 3 Green peppers
- 1 Large can crushed tomatoes
- 1 Bay leaf
- 5 Cloves garlic
- 8oz Vegetable broth
- 1 Can chickpeas
- 1 Can kidney beans
- 1 Can black beans
- 1lb Ground beef
- 1 Small tub ricotta cheese
- Fruit for lunch

Urgent

Appointment

Plan ahead or plan to fail

Important Notes

signs of the island being brought back to life anyway, I had

perfect

You are only one thought away from a good day.

Layer and layers of delicious!

7 Layer Banana Split

INGREDIENTS

- 1oz total: Shredded wheat, puffed kamut, uncooked oats (full grain)
- 2oz Plain Greek yogurt (1/2 protein)
- 1oz total: Sunflower kernels, cashews, walnuts, macadamia nuts, peanuts (1/2 protein)
- 6oz total: 1 Small banana, frozen blueberries, frozen strawberries (full fruit)
- Pinch of each: Nutmeg, sea salt, cinnamon, vanilla extract.
- 1/2oz Peanut butter (1/4 protein)

DIRECTIONS

1. Add frozen fruit and vanilla to a bowl and microwave 1min.
2. Slice banana the long way.
3. Layer banana, yogurt, fruit, nuts, grains, and seasonings.
4. Drizzle peanut butter on top

Bites of tuna salad heaven

Tunamatoe Bites

INGREDIENTS

- 6oz Tomatoes (full vegetable)
- 1oz Tuna (1/4 protein)
- 2oz Plain Greek yogurt (1/4 protein)
- 1/2oz Mayo (full fat)
- Pinch of each: Sea salt, pepper
- 1oz Cheese (1/2 protein)
- 2oz Pickles (condiment)

DIRECTIONS

1. Slice tomatoes and pickles.
2. In a separate bowl add tuna, Greek yogurt, mayo, seasonings, and mix.
3. Top tomato slices with cheese, pickles, and tuna mixture.

SIDE WITH 6OZ FRUIT FOR A COMPLETE LUNCH

Big ole bowl of chili!

Chili x2

INGREDIENTS

- 2lbs total: Onion, celery, green bell peppers, canned crushed tomatoes (full vegetable)
- 1 Bay leaf
- 1tsp Cumin
- 2Tbsp Oregano
- Sea salt, pepper
- 5 Cloves garlic
- 1Tbsp Chili powder
- 8oz Vegetable broth (condiment up to 8oz free)
- 6oz total canned: Kidney beans, chickpeas, black beans (1/2 protein)
- 4oz Ground beef (1/2 protein)
- 4oz Ricotta cheese (full fat)

DIRECTIONS

1. Brown ground beef.
2. Dice/chop garlic, onion, peppers, and celery.
3. Add onion, bay leaf, cumin, oregano, salt, and pepper to a large pot and sauté.
4. Add peppers, celery, broth, and browned beef.
5. Simmer 5min.
6. Add tomatoes, chili powder, and beans.
7. Bring to a boil, reduce heat to low.
8. Simmer 45min.
9. Remove bay leaf.
10. Divide chili into 2 bowls.
11. Top each bowl with 2oz ricotta cheese.
12. Refrigerate 1 bowl of chili for tomorrows dinner.

Day 9 done!

This way of eating really does work around your life and schedule. I have a pretty crazy and busy schedule (but I love it!) We run a teen night twice a month and it goes through supper time. It can be too hard to bring supper with us and eat it in a crunch time (some suppers are easy to pack and eat like chili, soups, and casseroles), but on those nights we will swap our lunch and dinner meals. So, we will have our dinner at home for lunch and bring our lunch and eat it for dinner. It works for us and since it's not an everyday thing it hasn't affected my weight loss. There are many times when we are going to a potluck or event that it's just easier to bring our own meal than guessing at portion sizes in the heat of the moment, and guess what? Nobody was bothered by it. So don't be pressured by what other's will think.

My Daily Gratitude

Today I'm grateful for

Daily Affirmation

Everyday and in everyway
I'm getting better and better
because of my Covenant with God

Kindness that I shared today

I learned today

WATER INTAKE

BREAKFAST:
1 GRAIN, 1 PROTEIN, 6OZ FRUIT

LUNCH:
1 PROTEIN, 1 FAT, 6OZ FRUIT,
6OZ VEGETABLES

DINNER:
1 PROTEIN, 1 FAT, 14OZ VEGETABLES

From my volume 8 cookbook

PLAN YOUR DAY

Today's Shopping List

- 1 Banana
- Spring mix lettuce
- 1 Onion
- 1 Cucumber
- Broccoli
- Frozen blueberries
- Feta cheese
- Red wine vinegar
- Lemon juice
- 1 Can black beans
- Raw or oven roasted walnuts

Urgent

Appointment

Plan ahead or plan to fail

Important Notes

signs of the island being brought back to life anyway, I had

You are only one thought away from a good day.

Blueberry Cobbler for breakfast?
Yes please

Blueberry Cobbler Oatmeal

INGREDIENTS

- 1oz Uncooked oats (full grain)
- 1oz Ricotta cheese (1/4 protein)
- 1/2oz Chia seeds (1/4 protein)
- 7oz Water
- Pinch of each: Sea salt, vanilla extract, cinnamon
- 4oz Plain Greek yogurt (1/2 protein)
- 6oz total: 1 Banana, frozen blueberries (full fruit)

DIRECTIONS

1. Mix oats, ricotta, chia seeds, water, salt, vanilla, and blueberries.
2. Microwave 2min.
3. Chop banana.
4. Stir banana into oatmeal.
5. Top oatmeal with yogurt and cinnamon.

Berries and walnuts on a salad
are a fabulous combination

Berry Walnut Salad

INGREDIENTS

- 6oz total: Spring mix lettuce, onion, cucumber, broccoli (full vegetable)
- 6oz total: Frozen blueberries, frozen strawberries (full fruit)
- 3oz Black beans or 1oz Feta cheese (1/2 protein)
- 1 1/2oz Walnuts (1/2 protein + full fat)

-Red wine vinaigrette

- 2oz Red wine vinegar
- 1oz Lemon juice
- 1tsp Dijon mustard
- 1/2tsp Basil
- Pinch of Garlic salt

DIRECTIONS

1. Chop vegetables.
2. Add spring mix to a large bowl and top with vegetables, frozen fruit, walnuts, and beans.
3. Add all vinaigrette ingredients to a bowl and mix. (there will be left over vinaigrette, which you can store in the fridge for later use.)
4. Drizzle with vinaigrette.

Left over chili.

Oh yeah, you did day 10!!!
This journey can be fun or a bummer, but it's your choice how you think it will be. There was a study done with a group of people who were to go out into society and take note of discrimination. They had a makeup artist who was going to put a large ugly scar on their face. But right as they were going to leave, the makeup artist said she needed to touch up their makeup. What she really did was remove the scar without them knowing it. The people went out, and came back saying, "People stared at us, laughed about us, whispered, and were so rude because of the scar." BUT THERE WAS NO SCAR! Life will go the way we perceive it. You are only one thought away from a good day. How you change that thought is with words. Say how you want life to be. Say the things you're thankful for. Because you are in control of your thoughts.

My Daily Gratitude

Today I'm grateful for

Daily Affirmation

I am happy, hopeful, and joyful

Kindness that I shared today

I learned today

WATER INTAKE

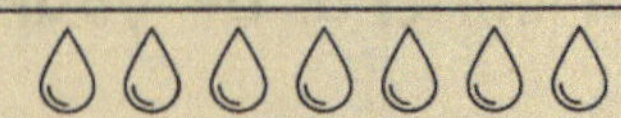

Something I am looking forward to tomorrow

habits I would like to change

New habits I would like to add

Kindness I can show tomorrow

Something I want to learn

BREAKFAST:
1 GRAIN, 1 PROTEIN, 6OZ FRUIT

LUNCH:
1 PROTEIN, 1 FAT, 6OZ FRUIT,
6OZ VEGETABLES

DINNER:
1 PROTEIN, 1 FAT, 14OZ VEGETABLES

From my volume 8 cookbook

PLAN YOUR DAY

Today's Shopping List

- Carton of eggs
- 2-3 Banana
- Flax seed
- Butter
- Sugar free BBQ sauce
- Napa cabbage
- 4oz Fruit for lunch
- Vegetables for lunch

Urgent

Appointment

Plan ahead or plan to fail

Important Notes

signs of the island being brought back to life anyway, I had

You are only one thought away from a good day.

Lemon blueberry heaven!!

Blueberry Lemon Breakfast Cheesecake

INGREDIENTS

- 2oz Lemon juice
- 4oz Plain Greek yogurt (1/2 protein)
- 1 Egg (1/2 protein)
- Pinch of each: Sea salt, vanilla extract, cinnamon, nutmeg
- 3oz Banana (1/2 fruit)
- 1oz Blueberries (1/6 fruit)
- 1oz Uncooked oats (full grain)
- 2oz Banana (1/3 fruit)

DIRECTIONS

1. Preheat oven to 350.
2. Mash 2oz banana.
3. Add oats, cinnamon, nutmeg, sea salt and mix.
4. Lightly oil a small baking dish.
5. Pour oat mixture into dish and cook 10min.
6. In a separate bowl, mash remaining banana.
7. Add remaining ingredients and mix.
8. Pour cheesecake mixture onto crust and bake 20min.
9. Cake will have a slight jiggle.
10. Refrigerate 4hr-overnight.

Donuts for lunch!

Cinnamon Donuts

INGREDIENTS

- 1/2oz Ground flax seed (1/4 protein)
- 1/2oz Peanut butter (1/4 protein)
- 2oz Banana (1/3 fruit)
- 1 Egg (1/2 protein)
- 1Tbsp Butter (full fat)
- 1/2tsp Baking powder
- 1Tbsp Cinnamon + more for topping
- 1/2tsp of each: Ginger, Sea salt

DIRECTIONS

1. Preheat oven to 350.
2. Mix all Ingredients.
3. Lightly oil a donut pan (muffin pan or a baking sheet works in making these as cookies or muffins also.)
4. Sprinkle each donut with more cinnamon and sea salt.
5. Bake 15min.

SIDE WITH 4OZ FRUIT AND 6OZ VEGETABLES FOR A COMPLETE LUNCH.

Donuts for lunch!

BBQ Chicken Wraps

INGREDIENTS

- 1oz Cheese (full fat)
- 3oz Cooked chicken (3/4 protein)
- 1oz Sugar free BBQ sauce (condiment)
- 7oz Napa cabbage (1/2 vegetable)
- 2oz Plain Greek yogurt (1/4 protein)

DIRECTIONS

1. Add cheese, chicken, and BBQ sauce to a bowl and mix.
2. Microwave mixture 1min.
3. Spread mixture onto cabbage and top with Greek yogurt.

SIDE WITH 7OZ VEGETABLES FOR A COMPLETE DINNER

Yay, day 11 comes to a close!
You are doing a fabulous job changing your habits and whole life. Now as time goes on there will be new challenges in life like going out to eat. There are many many options and it's not as scary as you would think.

#1. There is the 1 plate rule (depending on the size of the plate).

#2. You can play the game, "How close can I guess the weights of this food without my scale?"

#3. Bring your own packed meal (this works better for parties or fast food restaurants. I would not recommend doing this at a sit-down restaurant).

You can put together a compliant meal at almost any restaurant. Here is a list of my favorites and what I choose to order there.

Fast Food:

- Subway - Protein bowl, rotisserie chicken or any of their meat options, cheese, all the veggies, and the chipotle ranch for dressing (or they usually have balsamic vinegar).
- Taco John's - Taco salad without the shell and extra guacamole.
- Qdoba's or Chipotle - Salad bowl, beans, meat, extra fajita veggies, guacamole (2 scoops at Qdoba's), salsa, chipotle ranch dressing.

(Most fast food restaurants will have a salad option. Try to choose the ones without dried fruit or tortilla strips etc.)

Sit Down Restaurants:

- Applebee's or any Bar-N-Grill type - Burger without the bun (ask for a lettuce wrap instead), side salad instead of fries, and a side of vegetables, or look at their salad options.

- Mexican restaurants - Fajitas, no tortillas or rice, and extra of the pico and salad.

Buffets are a great option especially to get the dinner-sized portion of vegetables.

- Chinese Buffet - Grilled chicken, green beans, fish, I'll even pick out the veggies from the other food options, egg rolls (cut open and eat the insides), and they usually will have a salad bar also.
- Pizza Ranch (tread carefully) - Salad bar and then I will scrape off the top of the pizzas and not eat the crust.

Google is a great tool for searching salad bars, buffets, and looking at the menus.

For more info on eating out I vlogged our girls trip as we traveled and adventured restaurants and eating out. Find the vlogs >>>

My Daily Gratitude

Today I'm grateful for

Daily Affirmation

I am strong in the Lord and in the power of His might

Kindness that I shared today

I learned today

WATER INTAKE

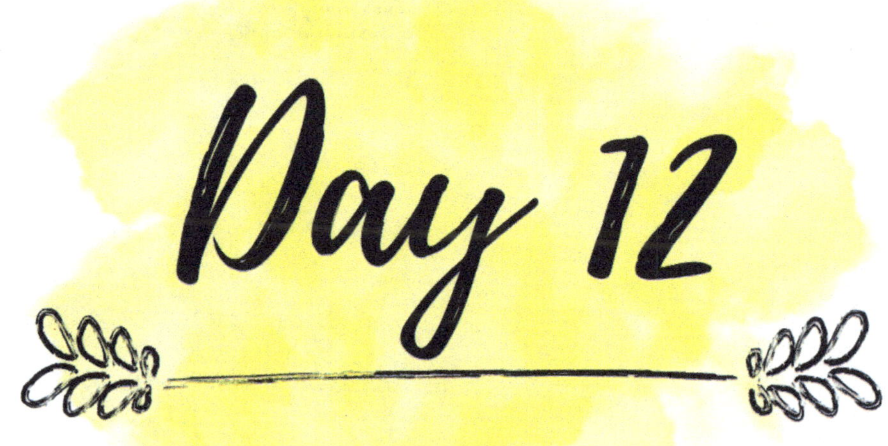

BREAKFAST:
1 GRAIN, 1 PROTEIN, 6OZ FRUIT

LUNCH:
1 PROTEIN, 1 FAT, 6OZ FRUIT,
6OZ VEGETABLES

DINNER:
1 PROTEIN, 1 FAT, 14OZ VEGETABLES

From my volume 9 cookbook

PLAN YOUR DAY

Today's Shopping List

- 1-2 Apples
- 6 Cloves garlic
- 1 Ginger
- 1 Can chickpeas
- 8oz Vegetable broth
- 6oz Frozen spinach
- 1 Small tub whole milk ricotta cheese
- 1 Orange
- 2 Banana
- 2 12oz Frozen carrots
- 2 Onions
- 2 12oz Frozen cauliflower rice
- Chicken breast
- Balsamic vinegar

Urgent

Appointment

Plan ahead or plan to fail

Important Notes

signs of the island being brought back to life anyway, I had

You are only one thought away from a good day.

apple Pie for breakfast is always a yes!!

Apple Pie Overnight Oats

INGREDIENTS

- 1oz Uncooked oats (full grain)
- 4oz Plain Greek yogurt (1/2 protein)
- 2oz Brewed coffee or water
- 1/4tsp Almond or maple extract
- 2oz Banana (1/3 fruit)
- 1/2tsp Cinnamon + more for topping
- 1/4tsp Nutmeg + more for topping
- Pinch of each: Ginger, allspice, sea salt
- 4oz Apple (2/3 fruit)
- 1/2oz Pecans (1/4 protein)
- 1/2oz Peanut butter (1/4 protein)

DIRECTIONS

1. Mash banana.
2. Mix 2oz Greek yogurt, banana, oats, coffee, almond extract, spices, and refrigerate overnight.
3. Chop apple.
4. Top oats with apple, cinnamon, nutmeg,
5. 2oz Greek yogurt, pecans, and drizzle with peanut butter.

Soup AND a parfait for lunch, and you thought you would be missing out by ditching sugar and flour.

Hulk Soup with Fruity Ricotta Parfait

INGREDIENTS

- 1oz Onion (1/6 vegetable)
- 2 Cloves garlic
- 2Tbsp Minced Ginger
- 6oz Canned chickpeas (full protein)
- 8oz Vegetable broth (condiment)
- Pinch of Sea salt
- 6oz Frozen spinach (shrinks to 5oz) (+ onion = full vegetables)
- 2oz Whole milk ricotta cheese (full fat)
- 6oz total: Orange, banana (full fruit)

DIRECTIONS

1. Dice onion and garlic.
2. Heat and lightly oil a small pot.
3. Sauté onion, garlic, and ginger.
4. Drain chickpeas.
5. Add chickpeas, vegetable broth and salt to your pot.
6. Bring to a boil.
7. Reduce heat and simmer 25min.
8. Add spinach and simmer 2min more.
9. Use a hand blender or pour soup into a blender, and blend until smooth.
10. Peel and cut orange into small pieces and slice banana.
11. In a separate bowl, add fruit, ricotta, and a pinch of salt to a bowl and mix

Easy throw together casserole yet packed with so many layers of flavor!

Chinese Chicken Caulirice Casserole x2

INGREDIENTS

- 2lbs total: Carrots, onion, cauliflower rice (shrinks to 14oz ea serving) (full vegetable)
- 2 Egg (1/2 protein)
- 4oz Cooked chicken (1/2 protein)
- 2Tbsp Sesame oil (full fat)
- 2tsp each: Apple cider vinegar, balsamic vinegar, parsley
- Pinch of each: Sea salt, pepper
- 1tsp Ginger
- 4 Cloves garlic

DIRECTIONS

1. Preheat oven to 375.
2. Mince garlic.
3. Add egg, vinegars, seasonings, garlic and oil to a bowl and whisk.
4. Add vegetables and chicken to a baking dish.
5. Pour in egg mixture and mix.
6. Bake 40min or until vegetables are tender.
7. Broil for 3min more.
8. Divide casserole into 2 servings.
9. Refrigerate 1 serving for tomorrows dinner.

Day 12 is conquered!

Only 2 days left until you have completed the whole 14 days of recipes! How are you feeling? More energetic, brain fog gone, cravings have subsided, and the new habits and routines are setting in? Are you discovering that this isn't as hard as you originally thought it would be? Because that's what I discovered. It was around this time that I thought, "You know what? I feel so good I could do this forever!" And that's exactly what I did! I will never regret making that decision and you won't either. Don't go back to the struggle and weight of carrying the excessive weight. Don't go back to having food rule over you and run your life! Stick with this freedom and new habits you have created. Your future self will thank you.

My Daily Gratitude

Today I'm grateful for

Daily Affirmation

I am a blessing going somewhere to happen

Kindness that I shared today

I learned today

WATER INTAKE

BREAKFAST:
1 GRAIN, 1 PROTEIN, 6OZ FRUIT

LUNCH:
1 PROTEIN, 1 FAT, 6OZ FRUIT,
6OZ VEGETABLES

DINNER:
1 PROTEIN, 1 FAT, 14OZ VEGETABLES

From my volume 9 cookbook

PLAN YOUR DAY

Today's Shopping List

- 3 Banana
- 1 Peanut butter
- 1 Can lentils
- 1 32oz Tub plain Greek yogurt
- Chicken breast
- Radish
- Cucumber
- Tomato
- Cabbage
- 1 Apple
- Grapes
- White wine vinegar

Urgent

Appointment

Plan ahead or plan to fail

Important Notes

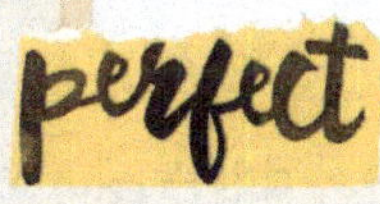

signs of the island being brought back to life anyway, I had

You are only one thought away from a good day.

warm banana bread covered in drizzly peanut butter, made in less than 10min!? what could be better than this!

Peanut Butter Banana Bread Mug Cake

INGREDIENTS

- 6oz Banana (Full fruit)
- 1 Egg (1/2 protein)
- 1oz Uncooked oats (full grain)
- Pinch of Sea salt
- 1/4tsp Baking powder
- 1oz Peanut butter (1/2 protein)
- Water

DIRECTIONS

1. Mash 3oz banana in a large mug.
2. Add 1/2oz peanut butter, egg, oats, salt, baking powder, and mix.
3. Microwave 3min or until a toothpick comes out clean.
4. Scrape a knife on the inside of the mug to loosen cake, tip mug over onto a place and lightly tap.
5. Slice remaining banana.
6. In a separate bowl mix remaining peanut butter and a splash of water.
7. Stir until smooth, repeat until peanut butter is drizzly.
8. Drizzle peanut butter on top of cake and side with banana slices.

Delicious protein packed Greek tossed salad.

Lentil Greek Chopped Salad

INGREDIENTS

- 3oz Canned lentils (1/2 protein)
- 2oz Plain Greek yogurt (1/4 protein)
- 1oz Feta cheese (full fat)
- 1oz Cooked chicken (1/4 protein)
- 6oz total: Spring mix lettuce, radish, cucumber, onion, tomato, cabbage (full vegetable)
- 6oz total: Apple, grapes (full fruit)

-Greek vinaigrette

- 1oz White wine vinegar
- 1tsp Dijon mustard
- 1/2oz Lemon juice
- 1tsp of each: Basil, Parsley, Oregano
- Pinch of Garlic salt

DIRECTIONS

1. Chop vegetables and fruit.
2. Add all vinaigrette ingredients to a bowl and mix.
3. In a separate bowl mix Greek yogurt and 1oz Greek vinaigrette.
4. Add all ingredients to a large bowl and toss/mix.

Left over casserolw for dinner.

13 Days done! You did it!!

Only 1 day left! One thing I learned in this weight loss journey that completely changed my whole way of thinking is...weight loss and life is not a sprint, it's a day in and day out choice of life. Don't get discouraged if you hop on the scale and the number hasn't moved. If you stick with this food plan IT WILL move. A weird thing about real weight loss is the scale numbers and the shrinking inches take turns. One day the scale will go down 3lbs but your clothes will still be tight. Then the scale will stall but your clothes will be baggier. Just relax and realize you are in this for the long haul so enjoy the journey, enjoy the little milestones, enjoy every size you go down, and celebrate the little victories all along the way like completing 13 whole days of no sugar and no flour AND no snacking!!

My Daily Gratitude

Daily Affirmation

I can do all things through Christ who strengthens me

Today I'm grateful for

Kindness that I shared today

I learned today

WATER INTAKE

Something I am looking forward to tomorrow
habits I would like to change
New habits I would like to add
Kindness I can show tomorrow
Something I want to learn

BREAKFAST:
1 GRAIN, 1 PROTEIN, 6OZ FRUIT

LUNCH:
1 PROTEIN, 1 FAT, 6OZ FRUIT,
6OZ VEGETABLES

DINNER:
1 PROTEIN, 1 FAT, 14OZ VEGETABLES

From my volume 10 cookbook

PLAN YOUR DAY

Today's Shopping List

- Paprika
- Salsa
- Hot sauce (franks hot sauce is my favorite)
- 1-2 Apples
- Potatoes or fries
- 1 Can chickpeas
- 1 Banana
- Cardamom
- Frozen berries
- 3-4 Zucchini
- Turkey pepperoni
- 1 Can black olives
- Spaghetti sauce
- Green olives
- Vegetables for lunch

Urgent

Appointment

Plan ahead or plan to fail

Important Notes

signs of the island being brought back to life anyway, I had

You are only one thought away from a good day.

Savory waffles to start your morning right.

Egg Waffle

INGREDIENTS

- 2 Eggs (weigh after cooking, eggs shrink to 2oz) (1/2 protein)
- Pinch of each: Paprika, parsley, garlic salt, onion powder, basil, sea salt, pepper, cinnamon
- 1oz Shredded cheese (1/2 protein)
- 2oz Salsa (condiment up to 2oz free)
- Hot sauce
- 6oz Apple
- 4oz Cooked potato fries or cooked potatoes (full grain)

DIRECTIONS

1. Heat and lightly oil a waffle maker.
2. Whisk eggs, 1/2oz cheese, and seasonings except cinnamon.
3. Pour mixture into waffle maker and cook 7-10min.
4. Top waffle with remaining 1/2oz cheese.
5. Slice apples.
6. Sprinkle apples with salt and cinnamon.
7. Side waffles with fries, hot sauce, salsa, and cinnamon apples.

Savory waffles to start your morning right.

PB&J Chickpea Crumble Pie

INGREDIENTS

- 3oz Canned chickpeas (1/2 protein)
- 1oz Peanut butter (1/4 protein +1/2 fat)
- 1oz Banana (1/6 fruit)
- Pinch of each: Baking powder, baking soda, sea salt, maple extract, cinnamon, cardamom
- 5oz Frozen berries (5/6 fruit)
- 2oz Plain Greek yogurt (1/4 protein)

SIDE WITH 6OZ VEGETABLES FOR A COMPLETE LUNCH.

DIRECTIONS

1. Preheat oven to 350.
2. Blend chickpeas and peanut butter.
3. Add banana, baking powder, baking soda, sea salt, maple extract and mix/mash.
4. Lightly oil a small pie tin or baking dish.
5. Scoop half of chickpea mixture into dish and flatten.
6. You can use parchment paper to help flatten your crust.
7. Top with berries and a liberal sprinkle of cinnamon and cardamom.
8. Crumble remaining chickpea mixture on top of berries.
9. Bake 20-25min.
10. Top with Greek yogurt.

Cheesy zucchini boats

Zucchini Pizza

INGREDIENTS

- 7oz Zucchini (weigh after baking) (1/2 vegetable)
- 1oz Turkey pepperoni (1/4 protein)
- 2oz total: Black olives, green olives (full fat)
- 1 1/2oz Shredded cheese (3/4 protein)
- 2oz Spaghetti sauce (condiment up to 2oz free)

SIDE WITH 7OZ VEGETABLES FOR A COMPLETE DINNER

DIRECTIONS

1. Preheat oven to 375.
2. Slice zucchini the long way.
3. Lightly oil a baking pan.
4. Place zucchini on pan and bake 25-30min.
5. Weigh zucchini and top with spaghetti sauce, pepperoni, cheese, and olives.
6. Bake another 10-12min or until cheese is melted.

Round of applause!!
You completed 14 days!!!
And you rocked it!!
You've got the hang of this now, so experiment with new recipes, discover your new favorites, and live life to the fullest with this newfound food freedom. To keep you inspired and strong on this lifelong journey, check out my other 25+ cookbooks including 2 Batch Cooking Made Easy which are packed full of deliciously easy recipes and real-life inspirational stories. Find my cookbooks, recipes, food galleries, and more on my website WeightLossRecipesCookbook.com.
For more mental peace and heart healing, check out my sister Kelly Aul's 2 Freedom From Food Addiction Devotionals. Find them on her website KellyAulNovels.com

My Daily Gratitude

Today I'm grateful for

Daily Affirmation

I am loved and I love

Kindness that I shared today

I learned today

WATER INTAKE

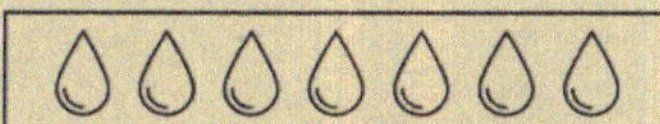

Something I am looking forward to tomorrow

habits I would like to change

New habits I would like to add

Kindness I can show tomorrow

Something I want to learn

Sauces, Seasonings, and Sides

Pumpkin Pie Spice

INGREDIENTS

- 2Tbsp Ground cinnamon
- 2tsp of each: Ground ginger, nutmeg
- 1tsp Ground cloves
- 1tsp Ground allspice

DIRECTIONS

1. Add all ingredients to a spice jar or container and mix.

Nothing tastes better than homemade

Taco Seasoning

INGREDIENTS

- 1cup Chili powder.
- 4tsp of each: Garlic powder, onion powder, crushed red pepper flakes, dried oregano
- 8tsp Paprika
- ½cup Cumin
- 1Tbsp of each: Sea salt, pepper

FIND THIS RECIPE ALSO IN MY VOLUME 1 COOKBOOK AND COOKING WITH JOY

DIRECTIONS

1. Add all ingredients to a spice container.
2. Shake/mix
3. Use 1Tbsp per 1lb of meat

One of my favorite seasonings!

Chipotle Seasoning

INGREDIENTS

- 1Tbsp of each: Onion powder, parsley, basil, garlic powder
- 1/2Tbsp Cumin
- 2tsp Chipotle pepper powder
- 1tsp of each: Sea salt, black pepper
- 1/2tsp Cayenne pepper

DIRECTIONS

1. Add all ingredients to a spice container.
2. Shake/mix

a warm seasoning

Chai spice

INGREDIENTS

- 2tsp of each: Cardamom, allspice, nutmeg, cloves
- 4tsp Cinnamon
- 6tsp Ginger

DIRECTIONS

1. Add all ingredients to a spice container.
2. Shake/mix

FIND THIS RECIPE ALSO IN MY VOLUME 9 COOKBOOK AND COOKING WITH JOY

The perfect seasoning for
EVERYTHING!

Seasoned Fry Spice

INGREDIENTS

- 2Tbsp of each: Garlic powder, onion powder, parsley
- 2 1/2Tbsp Paprika
- 2tsp Garlic salt

DIRECTIONS

1. Add all ingredients to a spice container.
2. Shake/mix

FIND THIS RECIPE ALSO IN MY VOLUME 13 COOKBOOK

A little about me.

Growing up I never knew how normal healthy people ate. I have been overweight since I was about 9 years old. I always felt insecure about my weight and eating around others. Then as a family, we changed our diets to whole, healthy foods... and I still was overweight (it is possible to eat healthy foods and still be overweight). We never gave up our Friday night junk foods though... Which slowly grew into Friday, Saturday junk food... Then into all weekend junk foods... And cravings all the rest of the week

As I grew up, I tried all the different kinds of diets with my mom and sister. They never lasted. The sugar and flour were always there... just waiting for us to fail... and we did. I even tried the keto diet and lost 10 pounds! But...I went right back to the old eating habits.

Until one day, my mom called my sister and I into her room. She showed us the first video to an amazing plan on Facebook. It talked about how this way of eating takes all the willpower out. (Which is what we needed!!)We three girls started and went all out. Once we started, we quickly found out that this is the best lifestyle- ever!

For a couple of years, God had been speaking to my mom and He told her, "Your influence for Me will not be as effective in society if you remain overweight. People will be more accepting and open if you will lose the weight." (Sadly, our society is very judgmental) So that's what we did. This has been the best lifestyle change. (it is not a diet). I have lost over 87lbs and have never felt better! The body insecurities are GONE! I don't have to think,

"What are they thinking about me. Do I look fat? Will I fit in that chair? I have to shop in the plus size section while all of my friends get to shop in the cute clothing sections." Now I can just throw on jeans and a t-shirt and I don't have to worry about my body or what I look like. I have so much energy. I don't have the tired headaches or the 'blec' feeling after eating junk food. I never have to feel insecure about eating food in front of other people. I can shop in the normal size people sections. I have never been this skinny in my whole life and I will never go back to the old me. Never! I'm not at my goal weight yet but I'm enjoying the journey. It is truly Deliciously Free!!

With Joy, Natalie

About the Author

Find all of my cookbooks, video's, recipes, recipe index, food galleries, and more on my website WeightLossRecipesCookbook.com

Natalie Aul

Picture from left to right. Tom-dad, Kelly-older sister, Maggie-mom, John, older brother, Natalie-me

Natalie was born and raised in Minnesota and was home-schooled along with her siblings. She works full-time with her family at Love of God Family Church in Fergus Falls, Minnesota, leading worship, singing, playing keyboard, and drums. She also writes skits and performs with the church's Blast Kids program.

Follow me on
Tiktok
Instagram
Facebook
Youtube
Pinterest
and more!

For daily inspiration,
updates, fun, and more

@ WeightLossRecipesCookbook

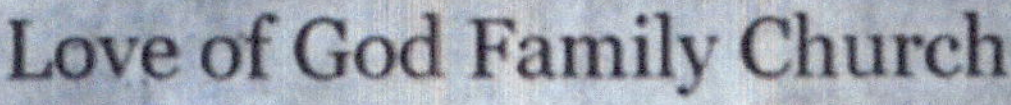

Loving God
His Word, His People

It's like coming home...

We're a family growing together in worship. We serve, laugh, play games, learn, and we share one another's victories and sorrows.

Our doors are open. Our hearts are open, also. If you're looking for a place to belong and grow close to God,

Welcome home!

Pastors Tom & Maggie Aul

Made in the USA
Coppell, TX
02 November 2023